Getting it Done.

To Do List
Daily Planner.

Activinotes

Activinotes

DAILY JOURNALS, PLANNERS, NOTEBOOKS AND OTHER BLANK BOOKS

A Daily Planner

DATE:

THINGS TO DO:

COMPLETED

☐
☐
☐
☐
☐
☐
☐
☐
☐
☐
☐
☐
☐
☐
☐
☐
☐
☐
☐
☐

COMMENTS: _____
_____
_____

A Daily Planner

DATE:

THINGS TO DO: **COMPLETED**

COMMENTS:

A Daily Planner

DATE:

THINGS TO DO: **COMPLETED**

COMMENTS: _____
_____
_____

A Daily Planner

DATE:

THINGS TO DO: **COMPLETED**

_____ ☐
_____ ☐
_____ ☐
_____ ☐
_____ ☐
_____ ☐
_____ ☐
_____ ☐
_____ ☐
_____ ☐
_____ ☐
_____ ☐
_____ ☐
_____ ☐
_____ ☐
_____ ☐
_____ ☐
_____ ☐
_____ ☐
_____ ☐
_____

COMMENTS: _____
_____
_____

A Daily Planner

DATE:

THINGS TO DO: **COMPLETED**

☐
☐
☐
☐
☐
☐
☐
☐
☐
☐
☐
☐
☐
☐
☐
☐
☐
☐
☐
☐
☐

COMMENTS: _____

_____

_____

A Daily Planner

DATE:

THINGS TO DO: **COMPLETED**

_____ ☐
_____ ☐
_____ ☐
_____ ☐
_____ ☐
_____ ☐
_____ ☐
_____ ☐
_____ ☐
_____ ☐
_____ ☐
_____ ☐
_____ ☐
_____ ☐
_____ ☐
_____ ☐
_____ ☐
_____ ☐
_____ ☐
_____ ☐

COMMENTS: _____
_____
_____

A Daily Planner

DATE:

THINGS TO DO:

COMPLETED

☐
☐
☐
☐
☐
☐
☐
☐
☐
☐
☐
☐
☐
☐
☐
☐
☐
☐
☐

COMMENTS: _____

_____

_____

A Daily Planner

DATE:

THINGS TO DO: **COMPLETED**

COMMENTS:

A Daily Planner

DATE:

THINGS TO DO: **COMPLETED**

COMMENTS: _____

A Daily Planner

DATE:

THINGS TO DO: **COMPLETED**

_____ ☐
_____ ☐
_____ ☐
_____ ☐
_____ ☐
_____ ☐
_____ ☐
_____ ☐
_____ ☐
_____ ☐
_____ ☐
_____ ☐
_____ ☐
_____ ☐
_____ ☐
_____ ☐
_____ ☐
_____ ☐
_____ ☐
_____ ☐
_____ ☐

COMMENTS: _____

_____
_____

A Daily Planner

DATE:

THINGS TO DO: **COMPLETED**

COMMENTS: _____

A Daily Planner

DATE:

THINGS TO DO: **COMPLETED**

_____ □
_____ □
_____ □
_____ □
_____ □
_____ □
_____ □
_____ □
_____ □
_____ □
_____ □
_____ □
_____ □
_____ □
_____ □
_____ □
_____ □
_____ □
_____ □
_____ □
_____ □

COMMENTS: _____

_____

_____

A Daily Planner

DATE:

THINGS TO DO: **COMPLETED**

☐
☐
☐
☐
☐
☐
☐
☐
☐
☐
☐
☐
☐
☐
☐
☐
☐
☐
☐
☐

COMMENTS: _____
_____
_____

A Daily Planner

DATE:

THINGS TO DO: **COMPLETED**

COMMENTS:

A Daily Planner

DATE:

THINGS TO DO: **COMPLETED**

COMMENTS: _____

_____

_____

A Daily Planner

DATE:

THINGS TO DO: **COMPLETED**

☐
☐
☐
☐
☐
☐
☐
☐
☐
☐
☐
☐
☐
☐
☐
☐
☐
☐
☐
☐

COMMENTS: _____
_____
_____

A Daily Planner

DATE:

THINGS TO DO: **COMPLETED**

_____ ☐
_____ ☐
_____ ☐
_____ ☐
_____ ☐
_____ ☐
_____ ☐
_____ ☐
_____ ☐
_____ ☐
_____ ☐
_____ ☐
_____ ☐
_____ ☐
_____ ☐
_____ ☐
_____ ☐
_____ ☐
_____ ☐

COMMENTS: _____
_____
_____

A Daily Planner

DATE:

THINGS TO DO: **COMPLETED**

COMMENTS:

A Daily Planner

DATE:

THINGS TO DO: **COMPLETED**

_____ ☐
_____ ☐
_____ ☐
_____ ☐
_____ ☐
_____ ☐
_____ ☐
_____ ☐
_____ ☐
_____ ☐
_____ ☐
_____ ☐
_____ ☐
_____ ☐
_____ ☐
_____ ☐
_____ ☐
_____ ☐
_____ ☐
_____ ☐

COMMENTS: _____
_____
_____

A Daily Planner

DATE:

THINGS TO DO: **COMPLETED**

A Daily Planner

DATE:

THINGS TO DO: **COMPLETED**

_____ ☐
_____ ☐
_____ ☐
_____ ☐
_____ ☐
_____ ☐
_____ ☐
_____ ☐
_____ ☐
_____ ☐
_____ ☐
_____ ☐
_____ ☐
_____ ☐
_____ ☐
_____ ☐
_____ ☐
_____ ☐
_____ ☐
_____ ☐

COMMENTS: _____

_____

_____

A Daily Planner

DATE:

THINGS TO DO:

COMPLETED

COMMENTS:

A Daily Planner

DATE:

THINGS TO DO:

COMPLETED

COMMENTS: _____
_____
_____

A Daily Planner

DATE:

THINGS TO DO: **COMPLETED**

	☐
	☐
	☐
	☐
	☐
	☐
	☐
	☐
	☐
	☐
	☐
	☐
	☐
	☐
	☐
	☐
	☐
	☐
	☐
	☐

COMMENTS: _____
_____
_____

A Daily Planner

DATE:

THINGS TO DO: **COMPLETED**

☐
☐
☐
☐
☐
☐
☐
☐
☐
☐
☐
☐
☐
☐
☐
☐
☐
☐
☐
☐
☐

COMMENTS: _____

_____

_____

A Daily Planner

DATE:

THINGS TO DO: **COMPLETED**

_____ ☐

_____ ☐

_____ ☐

_____ ☐

_____ ☐

_____ ☐

_____ ☐

_____ ☐

_____ ☐

_____ ☐

_____ ☐

_____ ☐

_____ ☐

_____ ☐

_____ ☐

_____ ☐

_____ ☐

_____ ☐

_____ ☐

_____ ☐

COMMENTS: _____

_____

_____

A Daily Planner

DATE:

THINGS TO DO: **COMPLETED**

_____ ☐
_____ ☐
_____ ☐
_____ ☐
_____ ☐
_____ ☐
_____ ☐
_____ ☐
_____ ☐
_____ ☐
_____ ☐
_____ ☐
_____ ☐
_____ ☐
_____ ☐
_____ ☐
_____ ☐
_____ ☐
_____ ☐

COMMENTS: _____

_____

_____

A Daily Planner

DATE:

THINGS TO DO: COMPLETED

COMMENTS: _____

_____

_____

A Daily Planner

DATE:

THINGS TO DO: **COMPLETED**

_____ ☐
_____ ☐
_____ ☐
_____ ☐
_____ ☐
_____ ☐
_____ ☐
_____ ☐
_____ ☐
_____ ☐
_____ ☐
_____ ☐
_____ ☐
_____ ☐
_____ ☐
_____ ☐
_____ ☐
_____ ☐
_____ ☐
_____ ☐
_____ ☐

COMMENTS: _____

_____

_____

A Daily Planner

DATE:

THINGS TO DO: **COMPLETED**

_____ ☐
_____ ☐
_____ ☐
_____ ☐
_____ ☐
_____ ☐
_____ ☐
_____ ☐
_____ ☐
_____ ☐
_____ ☐
_____ ☐
_____ ☐
_____ ☐
_____ ☐
_____ ☐
_____ ☐
_____ ☐
_____ ☐

COMMENTS: _____

_____

_____

A Daily Planner

DATE:

THINGS TO DO: **COMPLETED**

COMMENTS:

A Daily Planner

DATE:

THINGS TO DO: **COMPLETED**

_____   ☐
_____   ☐
_____   ☐
_____   ☐
_____   ☐
_____   ☐
_____   ☐
_____   ☐
_____   ☐
_____   ☐
_____   ☐
_____   ☐
_____   ☐
_____   ☐
_____   ☐
_____   ☐
_____   ☐
_____   ☐
_____   ☐
_____   ☐
_____   ☐
_____

COMMENTS: _____

_____

_____

A Daily Planner

DATE:

THINGS TO DO: **COMPLETED**

	☐
	☐
	☐
	☐
	☐
	☐
	☐
	☐
	☐
	☐
	☐
	☐
	☐
	☐
	☐
	☐
	☐
	☐
	☐

COMMENTS: _____

_____

_____

A Daily Planner

DATE:

THINGS TO DO: **COMPLETED**

_____ ☐
_____ ☐
_____ ☐
_____ ☐
_____ ☐
_____ ☐
_____ ☐
_____ ☐
_____ ☐
_____ ☐
_____ ☐
_____ ☐
_____ ☐
_____ ☐
_____ ☐
_____ ☐
_____ ☐
_____ ☐
_____ ☐
_____ ☐
_____ ☐
_____ ☐

COMMENTS: _____
_____
_____

A Daily Planner

DATE:

THINGS TO DO: **COMPLETED**

COMMENTS: _____
_____
_____

A Daily Planner

DATE:

THINGS TO DO: **COMPLETED**

_____ ☐
_____ ☐
_____ ☐
_____ ☐
_____ ☐
_____ ☐
_____ ☐
_____ ☐
_____ ☐
_____ ☐
_____ ☐
_____ ☐
_____ ☐
_____ ☐
_____ ☐
_____ ☐
_____ ☐
_____ ☐
_____ ☐
_____ ☐

COMMENTS: _____

_____

_____

A Daily Planner

DATE:

THINGS TO DO: **COMPLETED**

_____ ☐
_____ ☐
_____ ☐
_____ ☐
_____ ☐
_____ ☐
_____ ☐
_____ ☐
_____ ☐
_____ ☐
_____ ☐
_____ ☐
_____ ☐
_____ ☐
_____ ☐
_____ ☐
_____ ☐
_____ ☐
_____ ☐
_____ ☐

COMMENTS: _____

_____

_____

A Daily Planner

DATE:

THINGS TO DO: **COMPLETED**

_____ ☐
_____ ☐
_____ ☐
_____ ☐
_____ ☐
_____ ☐
_____ ☐
_____ ☐
_____ ☐
_____ ☐
_____ ☐
_____ ☐
_____ ☐
_____ ☐
_____ ☐
_____ ☐
_____ ☐
_____ ☐
_____ ☐
_____ ☐

COMMENTS: _____

_____

_____

A Daily Planner

DATE:

THINGS TO DO: **COMPLETED**

_____ ☐
_____ ☐
_____ ☐
_____ ☐
_____ ☐
_____ ☐
_____ ☐
_____ ☐
_____ ☐
_____ ☐
_____ ☐
_____ ☐
_____ ☐
_____ ☐
_____ ☐
_____ ☐
_____ ☐
_____ ☐
_____ ☐

COMMENTS: _____

_____

_____

A Daily Planner

DATE:

THINGS TO DO: **COMPLETED**

_____ ☐
_____ ☐
_____ ☐
_____ ☐
_____ ☐
_____ ☐
_____ ☐
_____ ☐
_____ ☐
_____ ☐
_____ ☐
_____ ☐
_____ ☐
_____ ☐
_____ ☐
_____ ☐
_____ ☐
_____ ☐
_____ ☐
_____ ☐

COMMENTS: _____
_____
_____

A Daily Planner

DATE:

THINGS TO DO: **COMPLETED**

COMMENTS: _____
_____
_____

A Daily Planner

DATE:

THINGS TO DO: **COMPLETED**

COMMENTS:

A Daily Planner

DATE:

THINGS TO DO: **COMPLETED**

COMMENTS: _____

_____

_____

A Daily Planner

DATE:

THINGS TO DO: COMPLETED

_____ ☐
_____ ☐
_____ ☐
_____ ☐
_____ ☐
_____ ☐
_____ ☐
_____ ☐
_____ ☐
_____ ☐
_____ ☐
_____ ☐
_____ ☐
_____ ☐
_____ ☐
_____ ☐
_____ ☐
_____ ☐
_____ ☐
_____ ☐
_____ ☐

COMMENTS: _____

_____

_____

A Daily Planner

DATE:

THINGS TO DO: **COMPLETED**

COMMENTS: _____

_____

_____

A Daily Planner

DATE:

THINGS TO DO:
                                                    COMPLETED

COMMENTS: _____
_____
_____

A Daily Planner

DATE:

THINGS TO DO: **COMPLETED**

_____ ☐
_____ ☐
_____ ☐
_____ ☐
_____ ☐
_____ ☐
_____ ☐
_____ ☐
_____ ☐
_____ ☐
_____ ☐
_____ ☐
_____ ☐
_____ ☐
_____ ☐
_____ ☐
_____ ☐
_____ ☐
_____ ☐

COMMENTS: _____
_____
_____

A Daily Planner

DATE:

THINGS TO DO: **COMPLETED**

COMMENTS: _____

_____

_____

A Daily Planner

DATE:

THINGS TO DO: **COMPLETED**

COMMENTS: _____
_____
_____

A Daily Planner

DATE:

THINGS TO DO: **COMPLETED**

COMMENTS: _____

A Daily Planner

DATE:

THINGS TO DO: **COMPLETED**

_____ ☐
_____ ☐
_____ ☐
_____ ☐
_____ ☐
_____ ☐
_____ ☐
_____ ☐
_____ ☐
_____ ☐
_____ ☐
_____ ☐
_____ ☐
_____ ☐
_____ ☐
_____ ☐
_____ ☐
_____ ☐
_____ ☐
_____ ☐

COMMENTS: _____
_____
_____

A Daily Planner

DATE:

THINGS TO DO: **COMPLETED**

_____ ☐
_____ ☐
_____ ☐
_____ ☐
_____ ☐
_____ ☐
_____ ☐
_____ ☐
_____ ☐
_____ ☐
_____ ☐
_____ ☐
_____ ☐
_____ ☐
_____ ☐
_____ ☐
_____ ☐
_____ ☐
_____ ☐
_____ ☐
_____ ☐

COMMENTS: _____
_____
_____

A Daily Planner

DATE:

THINGS TO DO: **COMPLETED**

_____ ☐
_____ ☐
_____ ☐
_____ ☐
_____ ☐
_____ ☐
_____ ☐
_____ ☐
_____ ☐
_____ ☐
_____ ☐
_____ ☐
_____ ☐
_____ ☐
_____ ☐
_____ ☐
_____ ☐
_____ ☐
_____ ☐
_____ ☐

COMMENTS: _____

_____

_____

A Daily Planner

DATE:

THINGS TO DO: **COMPLETED**

A Daily Planner

DATE:

THINGS TO DO: **COMPLETED**

☐
☐
☐
☐
☐
☐
☐
☐
☐
☐
☐
☐
☐
☐
☐
☐
☐
☐
☐

COMMENTS: _____

_____

_____

A Daily Planner

DATE:

THINGS TO DO: **COMPLETED**

_____ ☐
_____ ☐
_____ ☐
_____ ☐
_____ ☐
_____ ☐
_____ ☐
_____ ☐
_____ ☐
_____ ☐
_____ ☐
_____ ☐
_____ ☐
_____ ☐
_____ ☐
_____ ☐
_____ ☐
_____ ☐
_____ ☐
_____ ☐

COMMENTS: _____

_____

_____

A Daily Planner

DATE:

THINGS TO DO: **COMPLETED**

COMMENTS: _____
_____
_____

A Daily Planner

DATE:

THINGS TO DO: **COMPLETED**

COMMENTS: _____
_____
_____

A Daily Planner

DATE:

THINGS TO DO: **COMPLETED**

☐
☐
☐
☐
☐
☐
☐
☐
☐
☐
☐
☐
☐
☐
☐
☐
☐
☐
☐
☐

COMMENTS: _____
_____
_____

A Daily Planner

DATE:

THINGS TO DO: **COMPLETED**

_____ ☐
_____ ☐
_____ ☐
_____ ☐
_____ ☐
_____ ☐
_____ ☐
_____ ☐
_____ ☐
_____ ☐
_____ ☐
_____ ☐
_____ ☐
_____ ☐
_____ ☐
_____ ☐
_____ ☐
_____ ☐
_____ ☐
_____ ☐
_____ ☐

COMMENTS: _____

_____

_____

A Daily Planner

DATE:

THINGS TO DO: **COMPLETED**

_____   ☐
_____   ☐
_____   ☐
_____   ☐
_____   ☐
_____   ☐
_____   ☐
_____   ☐
_____   ☐
_____   ☐
_____   ☐
_____   ☐
_____   ☐
_____   ☐
_____   ☐
_____   ☐
_____   ☐
_____   ☐
_____   ☐
_____   ☐
_____   ☐
_____   ☐

COMMENTS: _____
_____
_____

A Daily Planner

DATE:

THINGS TO DO:

COMPLETED

COMMENTS:

A Daily Planner

DATE:

THINGS TO DO: **COMPLETED**

_____   ☐
_____   ☐
_____   ☐
_____   ☐
_____   ☐
_____   ☐
_____   ☐
_____   ☐
_____   ☐
_____   ☐
_____   ☐
_____   ☐
_____   ☐
_____   ☐
_____   ☐
_____   ☐
_____   ☐
_____   ☐
_____   ☐
_____   ☐
_____   ☐

COMMENTS: _____

_____

_____

A Daily Planner

DATE:

THINGS TO DO: **COMPLETED**

COMMENTS: _____
_____
_____

A Daily Planner

DATE:

THINGS TO DO: **COMPLETED**

COMMENTS: _____

_____

_____

A Daily Planner

DATE:

THINGS TO DO: **COMPLETED**

_____ ☐
_____ ☐
_____ ☐
_____ ☐
_____ ☐
_____ ☐
_____ ☐
_____ ☐
_____ ☐
_____ ☐
_____ ☐
_____ ☐
_____ ☐
_____ ☐
_____ ☐
_____ ☐
_____ ☐
_____ ☐
_____ ☐
_____ ☐

COMMENTS: _____
_____
_____

A Daily Planner

DATE:

THINGS TO DO: **COMPLETED**

_____ ☐
_____ ☐
_____ ☐
_____ ☐
_____ ☐
_____ ☐
_____ ☐
_____ ☐
_____ ☐
_____ ☐
_____ ☐
_____ ☐
_____ ☐
_____ ☐
_____ ☐
_____ ☐
_____ ☐
_____ ☐
_____ ☐
_____ ☐

COMMENTS: _____

_____

_____

A Daily Planner

DATE:

THINGS TO DO: **COMPLETED**

COMMENTS: _____
_____
_____

A Daily Planner

DATE:

THINGS TO DO: **COMPLETED**

_____ ☐
_____ ☐
_____ ☐
_____ ☐
_____ ☐
_____ ☐
_____ ☐
_____ ☐
_____ ☐
_____ ☐
_____ ☐
_____ ☐
_____ ☐
_____ ☐
_____ ☐
_____ ☐
_____ ☐
_____ ☐
_____ ☐
_____ ☐
_____ ☐

COMMENTS: _____
_____
_____

A Daily Planner

DATE:

THINGS TO DO: **COMPLETED**

COMMENTS:

A Daily Planner

DATE:

THINGS TO DO: **COMPLETED**

_____ ☐
_____ ☐
_____ ☐
_____ ☐
_____ ☐
_____ ☐
_____ ☐
_____ ☐
_____ ☐
_____ ☐
_____ ☐
_____ ☐
_____ ☐
_____ ☐
_____ ☐
_____ ☐
_____ ☐
_____ ☐
_____ ☐
_____ ☐

COMMENTS: _____
_____
_____

A Daily Planner

DATE:

THINGS TO DO: **COMPLETED**

COMMENTS: _____

_____

_____

A Daily Planner

DATE:

THINGS TO DO: **COMPLETED**

_____ ☐
_____ ☐
_____ ☐
_____ ☐
_____ ☐
_____ ☐
_____ ☐
_____ ☐
_____ ☐
_____ ☐
_____ ☐
_____ ☐
_____ ☐
_____ ☐
_____ ☐
_____ ☐
_____ ☐
_____ ☐
_____ ☐
_____ ☐

COMMENTS: _____
_____
_____

A Daily Planner

DATE:

THINGS TO DO: **COMPLETED**

COMMENTS:

A Daily Planner

DATE:

THINGS TO DO: COMPLETED

_____ ☐
_____ ☐
_____ ☐
_____ ☐
_____ ☐
_____ ☐
_____ ☐
_____ ☐
_____ ☐
_____ ☐
_____ ☐
_____ ☐
_____ ☐
_____ ☐
_____ ☐
_____ ☐
_____ ☐
_____ ☐
_____ ☐
_____ ☐

COMMENTS: _____
_____
_____

A Daily Planner

DATE:

THINGS TO DO: **COMPLETED**

COMMENTS: _____
_____
_____

A Daily Planner

DATE:

THINGS TO DO: **COMPLETED**

_____ ☐
_____ ☐
_____ ☐
_____ ☐
_____ ☐
_____ ☐
_____ ☐
_____ ☐
_____ ☐
_____ ☐
_____ ☐
_____ ☐
_____ ☐
_____ ☐
_____ ☐
_____ ☐
_____ ☐
_____ ☐
_____ ☐
_____ ☐

COMMENTS: _____

_____

_____

A Daily Planner

DATE:

THINGS TO DO: **COMPLETED**

COMMENTS: _____
_____
_____

A Daily Planner

DATE:

THINGS TO DO: **COMPLETED**

☐
☐
☐
☐
☐
☐
☐
☐
☐
☐
☐
☐
☐
☐
☐
☐
☐
☐
☐
☐

COMMENTS: _____
_____
_____

A Daily Planner

DATE:

THINGS TO DO: **COMPLETED**

COMMENTS: _____
_____
_____

A Daily Planner

DATE:

THINGS TO DO: **COMPLETED**

COMMENTS:

A Daily Planner

DATE:

THINGS TO DO: **COMPLETED**

COMMENTS: _____

A Daily Planner

DATE:

THINGS TO DO: COMPLETED

_____ ☐
_____ ☐
_____ ☐
_____ ☐
_____ ☐
_____ ☐
_____ ☐
_____ ☐
_____ ☐
_____ ☐
_____ ☐
_____ ☐
_____ ☐
_____ ☐
_____ ☐
_____ ☐
_____ ☐
_____ ☐
_____ ☐

COMMENTS: _____

_____

_____

A Daily Planner

DATE:

THINGS TO DO: **COMPLETED**

COMMENTS:

A Daily Planner

DATE:

THINGS TO DO: **COMPLETED**

_____   ☐
_____   ☐
_____   ☐
_____   ☐
_____   ☐
_____   ☐
_____   ☐
_____   ☐
_____   ☐
_____   ☐
_____   ☐
_____   ☐
_____   ☐
_____   ☐
_____   ☐
_____   ☐
_____   ☐
_____   ☐
_____   ☐
_____   ☐

COMMENTS: _____
_____
_____

A Daily Planner

DATE:

THINGS TO DO: **COMPLETED**

COMMENTS:

A Daily Planner

DATE:

THINGS TO DO: **COMPLETED**

COMMENTS: _____

A Daily Planner

DATE:

THINGS TO DO: **COMPLETED**

COMMENTS:

A Daily Planner

DATE:

THINGS TO DO: **COMPLETED**

☐
☐
☐
☐
☐
☐
☐
☐
☐
☐
☐
☐
☐
☐
☐
☐
☐
☐
☐
☐
☐
☐
☐
☐

COMMENTS: _____
_____
_____

A Daily Planner

DATE:

THINGS TO DO: **COMPLETED**

COMMENTS:

A Daily Planner

DATE:

THINGS TO DO:

COMPLETED

COMMENTS: _____

A Daily Planner

DATE:

THINGS TO DO: **COMPLETED**

☐
☐
☐
☐
☐
☐
☐
☐
☐
☐
☐
☐
☐
☐
☐
☐
☐
☐
☐
☐

COMMENTS: _____

_____

_____

A Daily Planner

DATE:

THINGS TO DO: **COMPLETED**

_____ □
_____ □
_____ □
_____ □
_____ □
_____ □
_____ □
_____ □
_____ □
_____ □
_____ □
_____ □
_____ □
_____ □
_____ □
_____ □
_____ □
_____ □
_____ □
_____ □

COMMENTS: _____
_____
_____

A Daily Planner

DATE:

THINGS TO DO: **COMPLETED**

COMMENTS: _____
_____
_____

A Daily Planner

DATE:

THINGS TO DO: **COMPLETED**

☐
☐
☐
☐
☐
☐
☐
☐
☐
☐
☐
☐
☐
☐
☐
☐
☐
☐
☐
☐

COMMENTS: _____
_____
_____

A Daily Planner

DATE:

THINGS TO DO: **COMPLETED**

COMMENTS: _____

_____

_____

A Daily Planner

DATE:

THINGS TO DO: **COMPLETED**

COMMENTS: _____

_____

_____

A Daily Planner

DATE:

THINGS TO DO: **COMPLETED**

☐
☐
☐
☐
☐
☐
☐
☐
☐
☐
☐
☐
☐
☐
☐
☐
☐
☐
☐
☐

COMMENTS:

A Daily Planner

DATE:

THINGS TO DO: **COMPLETED**

_____ ☐
_____ ☐
_____ ☐
_____ ☐
_____ ☐
_____ ☐
_____ ☐
_____ ☐
_____ ☐
_____ ☐
_____ ☐
_____ ☐
_____ ☐
_____ ☐
_____ ☐
_____ ☐
_____ ☐
_____ ☐
_____ ☐
_____ ☐

COMMENTS: _____
_____
_____

A Daily Planner

DATE:

THINGS TO DO: **COMPLETED**

COMMENTS: _____

A Daily Planner

DATE:

THINGS TO DO: **COMPLETED**

_____ ☐
_____ ☐
_____ ☐
_____ ☐
_____ ☐
_____ ☐
_____ ☐
_____ ☐
_____ ☐
_____ ☐
_____ ☐
_____ ☐
_____ ☐
_____ ☐
_____ ☐
_____ ☐
_____ ☐
_____ ☐
_____ ☐
_____ ☐
_____ ☐

COMMENTS: _____
_____
_____

A Daily Planner

DATE:

THINGS TO DO: **COMPLETED**

☐
☐
☐
☐
☐
☐
☐
☐
☐
☐
☐
☐
☐
☐
☐
☐
☐
☐
☐
☐

COMMENTS:

A Daily Planner

DATE:

THINGS TO DO: **COMPLETED**

_____   ☐
_____   ☐
_____   ☐
_____   ☐
_____   ☐
_____   ☐
_____   ☐
_____   ☐
_____   ☐
_____   ☐
_____   ☐
_____   ☐
_____   ☐
_____   ☐
_____   ☐
_____   ☐
_____   ☐
_____   ☐
_____   ☐
_____   ☐

COMMENTS: _____

_____

_____

A Daily Planner

DATE:

THINGS TO DO: **COMPLETED**

COMMENTS: _____
_____
_____